Use at least 5 of your spelling words in
all spelling words used in the story.

Spelling Test

Your Answers		Correct Spelling If Incorrect	
1		1	
2		2	
3		3	
4		4	
5		5	
6		6	
7		7	
8		8	
9		9	
10		10	
11		11	
12		12	
13		13	
14		14	
15		15	
16		16	
17		17	
18		18	
19		19	
20		20	

Extra Credit Spelling Words
Scramble

Name: _____

Date: _____

Let's put your puzzle solving skills to the test. Try unscrambling the words using the words in the box.

DEER	CHIMPANZEE	DOG	CAT	ANT	BEE
CAMEL	CROCODILE	ALLIGATOR	BEAR	CHICKEN	CHEETAH
BIRD	COW				

1. galloaitr   _ L _ _ _ A _ _ _

2. nat   A _ _

3. areb   B _ _ _

4. eeb   _ _ E

5. brid   B _ _ _

6. mcael   _ A _ _ _

7. cta   _ A _

8. ahhteec   C _ _ _ _ _ H

9. kncehic   _ H _ _ K _ _

10. zineaphcem   _ H _ _ _ A _ _ _ E

11. woc   _ _ W

12. rcilceood   _ _ _ _ _ _ _ L E

13. dere   _ _ _ R

14. gdo   _ O _

Write sentences using words from above:

1. ....

2. ....

3. ....

Use at least 6 of your spelling words in a short creative story. Underline all spelling words used in the story.

Spelling Test

Your Answers	Correct Spelling If Incorrect
1	1
2	2
3	3
4	4
5	5
6	6
7	7
8	8
9	9
10	10
11	11
12	12
13	13
14	14
15	15
16	16
17	17
18	18
19	19
20	20

Extra Credit Spelling Words
Scramble

Name: _____

Date: _____

Let's put your puzzle solving skills to the test. Try unscrambling the words using the words in the box.

MAY	APRIL	NOVEMBER	OCTOBER	MARCH	FEBRUARY
JUNE	JANUARY	JULY	SEPTEMBER	DECEMBER	AUGUST

1. anjyuar   _ _ N _ _ R _

2. burreayf   F _ _ _ U _ _ _

3. mrcah   M _ _ _ _

4. lapri   _ _ _ _ L

5. aym   _ _ Y

6. ejnu   _ _ _ E

7. ljyu   _ U _ _

8. ugatsu   A _ _ U _ _

9. ebprtesem   _ _ P T _ _ _ _ _

10. ctorebo   O _ T _ _ _ _

11. rbvmeneo   N _ _ _ M _ _ _

12. emecbdre   _ E _ _ _ B _ _

Write sentences using words from above:

1. ....

2. ....

3. ....

Use at least 8 of your spelling words in a short creative story. Underline all spelling words used in the story.

Spelling Test

Your Answers	Correct Spelling If Incorrect
1	1
2	2
3	3
4	4
5	5
6	6
7	7
8	8
9	9
10	10
11	11
12	12
13	13
14	14
15	15
16	16
17	17
18	18
19	19
20	20

Extra Credit Spelling Words Scramble

Name: _____

Date: _____

Let's put your puzzle solving skills to the test. Try unscrambling the words using the words in the box.

FROG	DAY	FISH	KANGAROO	KITTEN	HAMSTER
EAGLE	GOAT	DOLPHIN	HORSE	FLY	GIRAFFE
FOX	GOLDFISH	DUCK	ELEPHANT		

1. poinhdl   _ O _ P _ _ _

2. udkc   D _ _ _

3. leaeg   _ A _ _ _

4. pthleena   _ L _ _ _ A _ _

5. ifsh   _ _ _ H

6. yfl   _ _ Y

7. xof   _ O _

8. grof   F _ _ _

9. aegrffi   G _ _ A _ _ _

10. toag   G _ _ _

11. fohdsgil   G _ _ _ _ _ I _ _

12. meshatr   _ _ _ _ _ _ E R

13. rsoeh   _ _ _ _ E

14. ogorakan   _ A _ _ _ R _ _

15. ttkeni   _ I _ _ _ N

16. ayd   _ _ Y

Write sentences using words from above:

1. ....

2. ....

3. ....

Use at least 7 of your spelling words in a short creative story. Underline all spelling words used in the story.

Spelling Test

Your Answers	Correct Spelling If Incorrect
1	1
2	2
3	3
4	4
5	5
6	6
7	7
8	8
9	9
10	10
11	11
12	12
13	13
14	14
15	15
16	16
17	17
18	18
19	19
20	20

Extra Credit Spelling Words
Scramble

Name: _____

Date: _____

Let's put your puzzle solving skills to the test. Try unscrambling the words using the words in the box.

PIG	MONKEY	LION	PUPPY	PLANT	NATURAL
ORBIT	PLANETS	RABBIT	OWL	OCTOPUS	LOBSTER
NONLIVING	PANDA	LIVING			

1. olin   _ _ O _

2. lignvi   _ I _ I _ _

3. etrbsol   L _ B _ _ _ _

4. mykoen   M _ N _ _ _

5. rlnatua   _ _ T _ R _ _

6. ilvnognni   _ _ _ _ _ V I _ _

7. psotouc   _ _ _ O P _ _

8. oitbr   _ _ _ _ T

9. wlo   _ W _

10. pndaa   P _ _ _ _

11. igp   _ _ G

12. stlepna   _ _ _ N _ T _

13. atnlp   _ _ _ _ T

14. puypp   _ _ _ _ Y

15. bribta   R _ B _ _ _

Write sentences using words from above:

. ...

. ...

. ...

_____

Use at least 4 of your spelling words in a short creative story. Underline all spelling words used in the story.

Spelling Test

Your Answers	Correct Spelling If Incorrect
1	1
2	2
3	3
4	4
5	5
6	6
7	7
8	8
9	9
10	10
11	11
12	12
13	13
14	14
15	15
16	16
17	17
18	18
19	19
20	20

Extra Credit Spelling Words Scramble

Name: _____

Date: _____

Let's put your puzzle solving skills to the test. Try unscrambling the words using the words in the box.

SPACE	HERS	RIVER	SPIDER	HIGH	SEASONS
SHEEP	ROOT	SHARK	SNAKE	SQUIRREL	SCORPION
RAT	SEAL	SOIL	SNAIL		

1. rta   _ A _

2. erirv   _ _ V _ _

3. orot   _ O _ _

4. pnsrcioo   _ C _ _ _ _ _ N

5. sael   S _ _ _

6. saesson   S E _ _ _ _ _

7. hasrk   S _ _ _ _

8. hpese   S _ _ _ _

9. alnsi   S _ _ _ _

10. sknea   _ _ _ K _

11. sloi   _ O _ _

12. ceasp   _ _ A _ _

13. prseid   S _ I _ _ _

14. rsruielq   _ _ U _ _ _ _ L

15. ehrs   _ E _ _

16. hgih   _ I _ _

Write sentences using words from above:

1. ....

2. ....

3. ....

Use at least 5 of your spelling words in a short creative story. Underline all spelling words used in the story.

_____

_____

_____

_____

_____

_____

_____

_____

_____

_____

_____

_____

_____

_____

_____

_____

_____

_____

_____

Spelling Test

Your Answers		Correct Spelling If Incorrect

Your Answers

1 _____

2 _____

3 _____

4 _____

5 _____

6 _____

7 _____

8 _____

9 _____

10 _____

11 _____

12 _____

13 _____

14 _____

15 _____

16 _____

17 _____

18 _____

19 _____

20

Correct Spelling If Incorrect

1 _____

2 _____

3 _____

4 _____

5 _____

6 _____

7 _____

8 _____

9 _____

10 _____

11 _____

12 _____

13 _____

14 _____

15 _____

16 _____

17 _____

18 _____

19 _____

20

Extra Credit Spelling Words
Scramble

Name: _____

Date: _____

Let's put your puzzle solving skills to the test. Try unscrambling the words using the words in the box.

INTO	LIVE	HIM	JUST	KNOW	HOUSE
LIKE	LITTLE	JUMP	LONG	HIS	KEEP
KIND	HOW	LEARN			

1. mhi   _ I _

2. sih   _ _ S

3. useho   _ O _ _ _

4. hwo   H _ _

5. toin   _ N _ _

6. mjup   _ _ _ P

7. jstu   _ _ _ T

8. ekep   K _ _ _

9. kdni   K _ _ _

10. wonk   K _ _ _

11. alrne   _ E _ _ _

12. keli   _ _ K _

13. lieltt   L _ _ _ L _

14. evli   _ _ V _

15. lnog   L _ _ _

Write sentences using words from above:

1. ....

2. ....

3. ....

Use at least 10 of your spelling words in a short creative story. Underline all spelling words used in the story.

Spelling Test

Your Answers		Correct Spelling If Incorrect	
1		1	
2		2	
3		3	
4		4	
5		5	
6		6	
7		7	
8		8	
9		9	
10		10	
11		11	
12		12	
13		13	
14		14	
15		15	
16		16	
17		17	
18		18	
19		19	
20		20	

Extra Credit Spelling Words
Scramble

Name: _____

Date: _____

Let's put your puzzle solving skills to the test. Try unscrambling the words using the words in the box.

MUST	ONLY	MANY	NOW	MUCH	MAY
ONE	OLD	MORE	NICE	NEW	NOT
LOOK	MAKE	NINE			

1. olok   _ _ O _

2. mkea   M _ _ _

3. aymn   _ _ _ Y

4. amy   M _ _

5. oerm   _ O _ _

6. humc   _ _ C _

7. umts   _ U _ _

8. wen   _ _ W

9. eicn   _ I _ _

10. inne   _ I _ _

11. tno   N _ _

12. own   _ _ W

13. lod   O _ _

14. eno   _ N _

15. yonl   _ N _ _

Write sentences using words from above:

1. ....

2. ....

3. ....

Use at least 5 of your spelling words in a short creative story. Underline all spelling words used in the story.

Spelling Test

Your Answers	Correct Spelling If Incorrect
1	1
2	2
3	3
4	4
5	5
6	6
7	7
8	8
9	9
10	10
11	11
12	12
13	13
14	14
15	15
16	16
17	17
18	18
19	19
20	20

Extra Credit Spelling Words
Scramble

Name: _____

Date: _____

Let's put your puzzle solving skills to the test. Try unscrambling the words using the words in the box.

OTHER	OUR	PRETTY	PUT	PLEASE	RED
PLAY	PURPLE	OUT	RAN	RIGHT	PEOPLE
OVER	ORANGE	RAIN			

1. aegnor   _ _ A N _ _

2. htero   _ _ H _ _

3. uro   _ U _

4. tuo   _ U _

5. rove   _ _ E _

6. oeelpp   _ _ _ P _ E

7. pyal   _ _ A _

8. eespla   _ _ E _ _ E

9. ytretp   P R _ _ _ _

10. ppruel   _ U _ _ L _

11. upt   P _ _

12. nria   _ _ _ N

13. nar   R _ _

14. dre   R _ _

15. tirgh   _ _ _ _ T

Write sentences using words from above:

_____

_____

_____

Use at least 9 of your spelling words in a short creative story. Underline all spelling words used in the story.

Spelling Test

Your Answers	Correct Spelling If Incorrect
1	1
2	2
3	3
4	4
5	5
6	6
7	7
8	8
9	9
10	10
11	11
12	12
13	13
14	14
15	15
16	16
17	17
18	18
19	19
20	20

Use at least 14 of your spelling words in a short creative story. Underline all spelling words used in the story.

Extra Credit Spelling Words
Scramble

Name: _____

Date: _____

Let's put your puzzle solving skills to the test. Try unscrambling the words using the words in the box.

SAY	SEE	THANK	SOON	SHE	SAW
SEVEN	SMALL	SHOULD	SIX	TEN	THAN
RUN	SOME	SAID			

nru   R _ _

aisd   S _ _ _

asw   S _ _

ays   S _ _

ese   S _ _

seenv   _ _ V _ _

esh   _ H _

osudhl   S _ _ U _ _

9. xsi   _ I _

10. alsml   _ _ A _ _

11. esmo   _ O _ _

12. noos   _ _ O _

13. tne   _ _ N

14. hnta   _ _ _ N

15. tnkah   _ _ A _ _

Write sentences using words from above:

_____

_____

_____

Use at least 3 of your spelling words in a short creative story. Underline all spelling words used in the story.

_____

_____

_____

_____

_____

_____

_____

_____

_____

_____

_____

_____

_____

_____

_____

_____

_____

_____

Extra Credit Spelling Words
Scramble

Name: _____

Date: _____

Let's put your puzzle solving skills to the test. Try unscrambling the words using the words in the box.

THE	TOO	THESE	THAT	THIS	THEIR
TWO	THEY	THINK	THEM	THING	THEN
THREE	THERE				

1. atht   _ H _ _

2. het   T _ _

3. rhiet   T _ _ _ _

4. hemt   _ H _ _

5. neht   T _ _ _

6. teerh   _ _ E _ _

7. etehs   T _ _ _ _

8. ehty   _ _ _ Y

9. hting   _ _ I _ _

10. nhtik   _ _ _ N _

11. shti   T _ _ _

12. ehrte   _ _ _ E _

13. oto   _ O _

14. wot   T _ _

Write sentences using words from above:

_____

_____

_____

Use at least 5 of your spelling words in a short creative story. Underline all spelling words used in the story.

Spelling Test

Your Answers		Correct Spelling If Incorrect	
1		1	
2		2	
3		3	
4		4	
5		5	
6		6	
7		7	
8		8	
9		9	
10		10	
11		11	
12		12	
13		13	
14		14	
15		15	
16		16	
17		17	
18		18	
19		19	
20		20	

Use at least 7 of your spelling words in a short creative story. Underline all spelling words used in the story.

Spelling Test

Your Answers	Correct Spelling If Incorrect
1	1
2	2
3	3
4	4
5	5
6	6
7	7
8	8
9	9
10	10
11	11
12	12
13	13
14	14
15	15
16	16
17	17
18	18
19	19
20	20

Use at least 6 of your spelling words in a short creative story. Underline all spelling words used in the story.

_____

_____

_____

_____

_____

_____

_____

_____

_____

_____

_____

_____

_____

_____

_____

_____

_____

_____

Extra Credit Spelling Words
Scramble

Name: _____

Date: _____

et's put your puzzle solving skills to the test. Try unscrambling the words using the words in the box.

WHITE	WHERE	USE	WHY	WHEN	WENT
WAY	WERE	WALK	WAS	WANT	WITH
WHO	VERY	WHICH	WHAT		

. sue   _ S _   9. athw   W _ _ _

. eyrv   _ _ R _   10. wnhe   _ _ _ N

. alkw   W _ _ _   11. rhewe   _ _ _ R _

. atnw   _ A _ _   12. hihwc   W _ _ _ _

. aws   _ _ S   13. ehwti   W _ _ _ _

. awy   _ _ Y   14. ohw   _ H _

. tewn   _ E _ _   15. yhw   W _ _

. weer   _ E _ _   16. whit   _ _ _ H

rite sentences using words from above:

_____

_____

_____

Use at least 9 of your spelling words in a short creative story. Underline all spelling words used in the story.

Spelling Test

Your Answers		Correct Spelling If Incorrect	
1		1	
2		2	
3		3	
4		4	
5		5	
6		6	
7		7	
8		8	
9		9	
10		10	
11		11	
12		12	
13		13	
14		14	
15		15	
16		16	
17		17	
18		18	
19		19	
20		20	

Use at least 8 of your spelling words in a short creative story. Underline all spelling words used in the story.

Extra Credit Spelling Words
Scramble

Name: _____

Date: _____

et's put your puzzle solving skills to the test. Try unscrambling the words using the words in the box.

TIGER	YES	WOLF	TELESCOPE	ZEBRA	WRITE
YOURS	WORK	UNIVERSE	YELLOW	WORD	SURFACE
TURTLE	STAR				

. owdr _ _ R _

. rokw _ _ R _

. rwtie W _ _ _ _

. lwyoel _ E _ L _ _

. sey Y _ _

. oruys _ _ _ R _

. atrs S _ _ _

8. earcfsu _ _ _ _ _ C E

9. oeseptcel _ _ _ E _ _ _ _ E

10. gitre _ _ _ E _

11. eturtl _ _ R _ L _

12. eiuservn _ _ _ V _ R _ _

13. lwof _ _ _ F

14. arbze Z _ _ _ _

rite sentences using words from above:

_____

_____

_____

_____

Use at least 6 of your spelling words in a short creative story. Underline all spelling words used in the story.

Spelling Test

Your Answers	Correct Spelling If Incorrect
1	1
2	2
3	3
4	4
5	5
6	6
7	7
8	8
9	9
10	10
11	11
12	12
13	13
14	14
15	15
16	16
17	17
18	18
19	19
20	20

Use at least 6 of your spelling words in a short creative story. Underline all spelling words used in the story.

Spelling Test

Your Answers		Correct Spelling If Incorrect	
1		1	
2		2	
3		3	
4		4	
5		5	
6		6	
7		7	
8		8	
9		9	
10		10	
11		11	
12		12	
13		13	
14		14	
15		15	
16		16	
17		17	
18		18	
19		19	
20		20	

Use at least 9 of your spelling words in a short creative story. Underline all spelling words used in the story.

Extra Credit Spelling Words
Scramble

Name: _____

Date: _____

et's put your puzzle solving skills to the test. Try unscrambling the words using the words in the box.

BLUE	ARM	EARS	BACK	GREEN	GRAY
BLACK	YELLOW	RED	BROWN	PINK	PURPLE
ORANGE	WHITE				

. kclab   _ _ _ _ K

. bule   B _ _ _

. robnw   _ _ O _ _

. yrag   _ _ A _

. energ   _ _ _ E _

. nearog   _ _ A _ G _

. pkni   _ _ _ K

8. peplru   P _ _ _ L _

9. erd   R _ _

10. withe   _ H _ _ _

11. wloyel   _ E _ _ O _

12. mra   _ _ M

13. kacb   B _ _ _

14. srea   E _ _ _

rite sentences using words from above:

_____

_____

_____

_____

Use at least 8 of your spelling words in a short creative story. Underline all spelling words used in the story.

Use at least 3 of your spelling words in a short creative story. Underline all spelling words used in the story.

Extra Credit Spelling Words
Scramble

Name: _____

Date: _____

Let's put your puzzle solving skills to the test. Try unscrambling the words using the words in the box.

NOSE	HAIR	FACE	LEGS	FEET	HANDS
KNEES	SHOULDERS	FOOT	EYES	HEAD	NECK
MOUTH	FINGERS				

1. esye   E _ _ _

2. cefa   _ A _ _

3. ftee   _ _ E _

4. sfgrien   F _ _ _ _ R _

5. ootf   _ O _ _

6. ahri   _ _ _ R

7. ndsha   H _ _ _ _

8. eahd   _ _ _ D

9. esken   _ _ _ E _

10. elgs   _ _ G _

11. muhot   _ O _ _ _

12. ekcn   _ E _ _

13. nsoe   N _ _ _

14. hsdolrseu   _ _ _ U _ _ _ _ S

Write sentences using words from above:

1. ....

2. ....

3. ....

Use at least 9 of your spelling words in a short creative story. Underline all spelling words used in the story.

_____

_____

_____

_____

_____

_____

_____

_____

_____

_____

_____

_____

_____

_____

_____

_____

_____

_____

_____

Extra Credit Spelling Words
Scramble

Name: _____

Date: _____

Let's put your puzzle solving skills to the test. Try unscrambling the words using the words in the box.

THURSDAY	SKIN	WEDNESDAY	TEETH	TONGUE	TOOTH
MONDAY	FRIDAY	SUNDAY	TUESDAY	TOES	SATURDAY
STOMACH	THUMBS				

1. snki   _ _ I _

2. chamost   S _ _ M _ _ _

3. httee   _ _ _ _ H

4. bhsutm   T _ _ _ B _

5. oets   _ O _ _

6. ngteuo   _ O N _ _ _

7. ohott   _ _ _ T _

8. suaydn   _ U _ D _ _

9. adymno   _ O N _ _ _

10. atseydu   _ _ E _ _ _ Y

11. aeedwsydn _ _ D _ _ S _ _ _

12. tdhrusay   _ _ _ _ _ _ A Y

13. ryfdia   F R _ _ _ _

14. tadasryu   _ _ T _ _ _ _ Y

Write sentences using words from above:

1. ....

2. ....

3. ....

Use at least 5 of your spelling words in a short creative story. Underline all spelling words used in the story.

Spelling Test

Your Answers

1
2
3
4
5
6
7
8
9
10
11
12
13
14
15
16
17
18
19
20

Correct Spelling If Incorrect

1
2
3
4
5
6
7
8
9
10
11
12
13
14
15
16
17
18
19
20

Semester Planner

Week	Monday	Tuesday	Wednesday	Thursday	Friday
1					
2					
3					
4					
5					
6					
7					
8					
9					
10					
11					
12					
13					
14					
15					
16					
17					
18					

Notes

Class: _____

		Week:					Week:					Week:					Week:			
Day		M	T	W	Th	F	M	T	W	Th	F	M	T	W	Th	F	M	T	W	Th	F
Date																						
Assignments																						
Name																						
	1																					
	2																					
	3																					
	4																					
	5																					
	6																					
	7																					
	8																					
	9																					
	10																					
	11																					
	12																					
	13																					
	14																					
	15																					
	16																					
	17																					
	18																					
	19																					
	20																					
	21																					
	22																					
	23																					
	24																					
	25																					
	26																					
	27																					
	28																					
	29																					
	30																					
	31																					
	32																					

Semester Planner

Week	Monday	Tuesday	Wednesday	Thursday	Friday
1					
2					
3					
4					
5					
6					
7					
8					
9					
10					
11					
12					
13					
14					
15					
16					
17					
18					

Notes

Class: _____

		Week:					Week:					Week:					Week:				
Day		M	T	W	Th	F	M	T	W	Th	F	M	T	W	Th	F	M	T	W	Th	F
Date																					
Assignments																					
Name																					
	1																				
	2																				
	3																				
	4																				
	5																				
	6																				
	7																				
	8																				
	9																				
	10																				
	11																				
	12																				
	13																				
	14																				
	15																				
	16																				
	17																				
	18																				
	19																				
	20																				
	21																				
	22																				
	23																				
	24																				
	25																				
	26																				
	27																				
	28																				
	29																				
	30																				
	31																				
	32																				

Made in the USA
Las Vegas, NV
09 October 2021